# IELTS

## Task 2 Writing - 7 or above

A self-study reference and practice book with model essays

**IELTSedits**

# IELTS

## Task 2 Writing - 7 or above

A self-study reference and practice book with model essays

**IELTSedits**

All rights reserved

Copyright © 2017 by IELTSedits

No part of this book may be reproduced or transmitted in any form or by any means, electronic or mechanical, including photocopying, recording or by any information storage and retrieval system, without the written permission of the publisher, except where permitted by law.

ISBN: 978 - 0 - 9933668 - 4 - 0

For further information e-mail the IELTSedits team at: ieltsedits@gmail.com

# The IELTSedits Team

The IELTSedits team is also able to help IELTS students wanting to further improve not only their vocabulary. but other IELTS exam skills.

## IELTS Writing

As one of the more difficult IELTS skills to master, it takes time to develop the experience needed to get grade 7.0 and above in writing.

However, IELTSedits offers you the chance to help your writing skills improve more quickly.

With many years of combined experience (including IELTS examining) the IELTSedits team offers you the chance to really learn how to write IELTS tasks the way the examiner wants to see them.

We not only offer lots of writing tips but we can also suggest ways for you to improve by sending you a Student Report for every writing task you write.

# SEND US YOUR ESSAYS TO GRADE

For more information write to the IELTSedits team at - **ieltsedits@gmail.com**

# Contents

|  | Page number |
|---|---|
| **PART I** | |
| Let's Start | 1 |
| Let's Start - Answers | 2 - 3 |
| Essay Topics | 4 - 7 |
| Essay Types | 8 |
| Essay Types - Structures/Opinion led | 9 |
| Essay Types - Practice | 10 - 11 |
| Essay Types - Structures/Argument led | 12 |
| Essay Types - Practice | 13 |
| Essay Types - Structures/Two questions | 14 |
| Essay Types - Practice | 15 |
| Paragraphs | 16 |
| Writing an Introduction | 17 |
| Introduction - Analysis | 18 |
| Introduction - information | 19 - 20 |
| Introduction - paraphrasing | 21 - 22 |
| Introduction - examples | 23 |
| Opinion led - introduction examples | 24 |
| Opinion led - examples analyzed | 25 |
| Argument led - introduction examples | 26 |
| Argument led - examples analyzed | 27 |
| Two questions - introduction examples | 28 |
| Two questions - examples analyzed | 29 |
| Getting Ready to Write | 30 |
| Writing Practice - 1 | 31 |
| Writing Practice - 2 | 32 |

# Contents

                                              Page number

**PART II**

| | |
|---|---|
| Brainstorming | 35 |
| Brainstorming by Googling | 36 - 37 |
| Writing Practice - 3 and 4 | 38 - 39 |
| Cohesive Phrases | 40 - 41 |
| Introduction | 42 - 44 |
| Introduction/TIME | 45 |
| Writing Practice - 5 and 6 | 46 - 47 |
| Main Body | 48 - 49 |
| Topic Sentences | 50 - 52 |
| Essay Analysis | 53 - 57 |
| Writing Practice - 7 and 8 | 58 - 59 |
| Expressing Positive / Negative Effects | 60 |
| Solutions | 61 |
| Cause and Effects | 62 |
| Conclusion | 63 |
| Writing Practice - 9 and 10 | 64 - 65 |
| Writing Practice - Model Answers 1 - 10 | 66 - 75 |
| Writing Test Score Sheet | 76 |
| ANSWERS | 78 - 79 |

# PART I

# Let's Start

Although this book is intended for students with some experience of writing Task 2 essays, it is still a good idea to go back to basics to refresh our minds of what can often be overlooked or not seen as important.

**Exercise**
Read the questions below and write answers to them on a separate sheet of paper.

1. What is the minimum length of a Task 2 essay?

2. How long should it take you to write a Task 2 essay?

3. What are the possible dangers of writing a much longer essay than the minimum?

4. How many paragraphs should you use?

5. How many essay types are there?

6. What are they?

7. What topics might you get to write about?

8. What makes a good essay?

9. What is the examiner looking for in an essay?

10. How are your essays graded?

# Let's Start - Answers

1. **What is the minimum length of a Task 2 essay?**
   250 words.

2. **How long should it take you to write a task 2 essay?**
   Forty minutes is the suggested time but if you take longer you then have less than twenty minutes for Task 1.

3. **What are the possible dangers of writing a much longer essay than the minimum?**
   One danger is that you might run out of time. An essay with no conclusion or very short conclusion will probably have a lower grade for Task Response. The examiner also likes to see signs of the ability to write in a clear concise manner but over developed ideas suggest the opposite.

4. **How many paragraphs should you use?**
   All of the essays here are based on four paragraphs.

5. **How many essay types are there?**
   There are three main essay types.

6. **What are they?**
   - Opinion led
   - Argument led
   - Two questions

7. **What topics might you get to write about?**
   Education / Technology / Environment / Society
   Health / Globalisation / Culture

   These are some of the common topics you will see but others are possible and it is important to become as familiar with as many possible Task 2 topics as you can.

8. **What makes a good essay?**

   - A minimum of 250 words.
   - The essay follows the correct topic and essay style.
   - Good range of vocabulary specific to the topic.
   - Words, phrases or ideas are repeated only when needed.
   - Good spelling.
   - Good use of cohesive phrases.
   - Good grammar with a mix of simple and complex sentence structures.
   - Correct use of paragraphs. (e.g. a gap between each paragraph)
   - A good conclusion.
   - And others (can you think of anything else?)

# Let's Start - Answers

## 9. What is the examiner looking for in an essay?

- Task Response

- Coherence and Cohesion

- Lexical resource (vocabulary)

- Grammatical Range and Accuracy (grammar)

## 10. How are your essays graded?
The grades from the four criteria are added together to form the final grade for the Task 2 essay. For example:

$$6666 = \text{grade } 6.0$$
$$6667 = \text{grade } 6.0$$
$$6677 = \text{grade } 6.5$$
$$6777 = \text{grade } 6.5$$
$$7777 = \text{grade } 7.0$$

**There are no half grades for the individual criterion**

# Essay Topics

The range of topics used for the Task 2 essay is quite varied. The list here is not complete (and never can be) as the list keeps changing with more topics added over time. Nevertheless, as you look at the list below, you will begin to get a good idea of the type of topics you might see in your IELTS test.

One topic can be developed into a number of possible essays with some topics possibly overlapping with other topics. For example, - health/food and diet - can easily be linked together to form other essays.

No attempt here has been given to present the exact Task 2 topic information as these can be searched for online on many different IELTS websites and many examples will be shown later in this book for you to practice your writing skills. The purpose of the listings here is simply to show you a selection of topics and the kind of directions they can be taken in. Hopefully, this helps to stir your creative juices and encourages you to think more and more about the kind of essays that you might write.

**Art**
Governments should support art.
Art is an important part of culture.
Art does not need to be taught at school.
Artists should be sponsored by the government.
Artists should be free to express anything they want.

**Business and Money**
Governments should control how much people earn.
More and more people are buying things online.
Rich countries are getting richer and poor countries are getting poorer.
Most people are in debt because of credits cards.
The best business people are those who can work in a team.

**Communications and Personality**
Famous people are more famous for their glamour and wealth than achievements.
Face-to-face communication is becoming a thing of the past.
Technology is taking away the need to talk face-to-face.
What problems can children face when using the Internet?
Are our personalities due to nature or nurture?

**Crime and Punishment**
Advanced technology is helping to reduce the crime rate in many cities in the world.
Most criminals reoffend once released from prison.
Violence in the media encourages juvenile crimes.
Teenagers should receive adult punishments.
Many people think women should not work in the police force.

# Essay Topics

## Culture
Traditional cultures will be lost as technology continues to develop.
Cultures are becoming more and more alike because of global brands.
Multi-cultural societies are more exciting and develop more quickly.

## Education
It is common for students to take a gap year after high school.
Discipline is becoming a bigger and bigger problem in schools.
Some people think children should not have homework everyday.
Schools should not teach art or music but focus on science and IT.
Some parents think children should do more educational activities in their free time.

## Environment
Some people say governments spend too much money protecting wildlife.
Increasing the cost of fuel will solve the environmental problems in the world.
Governments should help introduce an international car-free day.
More money should be spent on global warming than local environmental issues.
It is better to spend money on health care than protect animals.

## Family and Children
Some people feel it is better for children to grow up in the city.
Children should look after their elderly parents and not send them to a centre.
Children should be encouraged to watch TV as it is very educational.
The main responsibility of parents is to teach their children right from wrong.
In many western countries many couples are choosing to have no children.

## Food and Diet
The media often shows a healthy woman as being very thin.
Many processed foods and ready-made meals contain preservatives.
Should everyone become vegetarian?
Many people feel that the government should put heavy taxes on fast foods.
A child's diet today will affect their health in the future.

## Globalisation
Globalisation affects the world's economies in a positive way.
Transportation and communication are making the world look the same.

## Government
The government should increase spending on defence to ensure public safety.
The government should give more money to education and less to the arts.
Only the government can make significant changes in society.
The government should sponsor creative people such as artists and musicians.

# Essay Topics

### Health
The prevention of health issues is better than treatment and medication.
We are heading towards a health crisis due to our dietary habits.
Schools should have more mandatory exercise classes to help reduce obesity.
Public health is the responsibility of the government not the individual.
Walking is meant to be a perfect exercise yet less and less people are walking.

### Housing
In some countries people prefer to rent rather than buy a home.
Many countries need to build more homes due to a population explosion.

### Language
Learning a foreign language is a waste of time because computers can now translate.
In the future, people will decide to speak one global language.
Some people think you need to speak the language to know the culture.
You need to live or work in a country to learn that language fluently.

### Leisure
More money and less free time is better than less money and more free time.

### Media and Advertising
Some people think what children watch on TV affects their behaviour.
Some companies sponsor sports players as a way to advertise their products.
Violence in the media means violence in society.
Some people think that the news is too depressing and needs good news as well.

### Reading
There will soon be no need for public libraries as books will be available online.
Libraries should focus more on digital material rather than paper books.
E-books will eventually mean that no one will buy paper books.
The earlier children learn to read the better they perform in later life.

### Society
Many countries hope to improve by focusing on economic development.
Many women are now financially independent so they do not need to marry.
The best way to help homeless people is to give them money.
Financial aid is no longer seen as the best way to help developing countries.

### Space Exploration
Some governments are wasting money on space research.

# Essay Topics

### Sport and Exercise
Some people think dangerous sports should be banned.
Some people think sports teach children how to compete.
Sports stars should be good role models.
With increasing obesity universities should make sport compulsory for all students.

### Technology
Technology devices, like mobile phones, are making people less social.
Technology is increasing the gap between rich and poor.
Playing video games is not good for a child's mental health.
Too many technological devices can help ruin family relationships.
Unsupervised use of the Internet can put children at risk.

### Tourism
There is an ever growing demand for more flights because of increasing tourism.
Tourism should be banned to protect local cultures.
As a result of tourism, many historical buildings and sites are being destroyed.
Tourism has helped English become the dominant language in the world.

### Transport
The volume of traffic is a serious problem in many cities in the world.
People should be encouraged to live in cities to help solve the traffic problem.
Should the government invest more in the development of roads or railways?
One way to help congestion is to increase the tax on vehicles.
Some people think drivers should be forced to take a driving test every five years.

### Work
Some employers want to contact their staff all the time, even during holidays.
More and more people are stopping farming and moving to the cities.
Many people find it hard to balance their work with other parts of their life.
Finding job satisfaction is considered a luxury in many developing countries.
Having a good university degree guarantees people a good job.

**NOTE:** The exact way to write any of the topics here can only be decided when the complete Task 2 information is given AND the Task 2 instructions are also given. However, this list of topics can help to arouse your interest in what is happening in the world. Listen to the news, read magazines and newspaper, think about these topics and begin to develop your ideas about them. This will help you when you start to write an essay and have to brainstorm for ideas.

# Essay Types

You now know that there are many different essay topics for you to practice but the way you structure each essay is based not on the topic but the Task 2 instructions that you are given.

You need to know the structure for each essay type and practice enough so that you do not get the types mixed up. It is very common for a student to turn one essay type into another essay type and if this happens you can expect a lower grade than you deserve for Task Response.

These instructions can be divided into three main essay types:

**Opinion led** - in this type of essay you are always asked a direct question

**Argument led** - in this type of essay no direct question is asked

**Two questions** - in this type of essay you are always asked two questions

Exercise
Try to put the typical Task 2 instructions below with the correct essay type. Put the correct numbers into the correct column.

| Opinion led | Argument led | Two questions |
|---|---|---|
|  |  |  |
|  |  |  |
|  |  |  |
|  |  |  |

1. Advantages / Disadvantages
2. Cause / Solution
3. Discuss both points of view and give your own opinion
4. Discuss the advantages and disadvantages and give your own opinion
5. Do the advantages outweigh the disadvantages?
6. Do you agree or disagree?
7. Opinion / Solution
8. Problem / Solution
9. To what extent do you agree or disagree?
10. What is your opinion?

**NOTE:** If you are not clear what a "direct question" is then simply look at the end of the sentence. If there is a question mark then this is a direct question. **Answers on page 78.**

# Essay Types - Structures

You are going to learn about the structures needed for each of the three essay types. Within each essay type you will find the structure used is either the same or nearly the same for all of the different instruction variations used.

## Opinion led

**Paragraph 1 - introduction**
Your answer to the Task 2 question **MUST** be added to this paragraph. You can make this the last sentence in the paragraph. Before that use 1 to 2 sentences rephrasing the topic from the Task 2 introduction information.

Examples of answers to the Task 2 question that you can use as your opinion are as follows:

**Do you agree or disagree?**
I agree that children should start to learn a foreign language in primary not secondary school.

**To what extent do you agree or disagree?**
I completely disagree with the notion that all high school students should study how to be a good parent at school.

**Do the advantages outweigh the disadvantages?**
I am convinced that the disadvantages of free entry to museums outweigh any advantages.

**What is your opinion?**
I feel that both the individual and government are responsible for making improvements to the environment.

**Paragraph 2 – main body**
Now develop your argument explaining why you hold this particular point of view.

**Paragraph 3 – main body**
Develop another idea that also helps support your opinion.

In both main body paragraphs just give YOUR opinion. Do not try to guess what other people think and then try to argue against those opinions.

**NOTE:** you have only been asked for your opinion and so writing about the opinions of other people puts you very close to being off topic and lowering your grade for Task Response. Only do this if you - partly agree/disagree - rather than - completely agree/disagree.

**Paragraph 4 – final paragraph**
It is better to start ALL final paragraphs with – In conclusion – followed by a repeating of the opinion that you presented in the introduction. The final paragraph should **summarise** the reasons you have this opinion and then give a final opinion or recommendation.

# Essay Types - Practice

## Do you agree or disagree?

Depending on your level of confidence at this point in the book, you can use these practice essays in various ways. You can either use them as simply a reference of this type of essay (and come back to them later and write a complete essay), underline what information you feel is important and needs to be in your essay, write only the introduction or write the whole essay.

**1.**
Some people believe that arts like music and paintings should not be funded by the government. Others believe that these are important for a society and need government funding.

Do you agree or disagree ?

**2.**
Lying is always wrong, no matter whether it is a big lie or a white lie.

Do you agree or disagree?

**3.**
Testing on animals is common practice for products such as cosmetics or drugs. Some people regard testing on animals as completely wrong and inhumane and they believe it should not be allowed.

Do you agree or disagree with this statement?

**4.**
Computers have made it possible for office workers to do much of their work from home instead of working in offices every day. Working from home should be encouraged as it is good for workers and employers.

Do you agree or disagree?

**5.**
Nowadays, many students have the opportunity to study for part or their entire course in foreign countries. While studying abroad brings many benefits to individual students, it also has a number of disadvantages.

Do you agree or disagree?

**6.**
Governments around the world spend too much money on treating illnesses and diseases and not enough on health education and prevention.

Do you agree or disagree with this statement?

# Essay Types - Practice

## To what extent do you agree or disagree?

Depending on your level of confidence at this point in the book, you can use these practice essays in various ways. You can either use them as simply a reference of this type of essay (and come back to them later and write a complete essay), underline what information you feel is important and needs to be in your essay, write only the introduction or write the whole essay.

**1.**
Popular events like the World Cup for football and other international sporting occasions are essential in easing international tension and releasing patriotic emotions in a safe way.

To what extent do you agree or disagree with this opinion?

**2.**
Creative artists should always be given freedom to express their own ideas (in words, pictures, music, films) in whichever way they wish. There should be no governmental restrictions on what they do.

To what extent do you agree or disagree with this opinion?

**3.**
Most developed countries spend a large proportion of their health budgets on expensive medical technology and procedures. This money should be spent instead on health education to keep people well.

To what extent do you agree or disagree?

**4.**
In many countries today the eating habits and lifestyle of children are different from those of previous generations. Some people say this has had a negative effect on their health.

To what extent do you agree or disagree?

**5.**
Our modern lifestyle means that many parents have little time for their children. Many children suffer because they don't get as much attention from their parents as children did in the past.

To what extent do you agree or disagree?

**6.**
Nowadays, people work hard to buy more things. This has made our lives generally more comfortable, but many traditional values and customs have been lost and this is a pity.

To what extent do you agree or disagree?

# Essay Types - Structures

## Argument led

**Paragraph 1 – introduction**
You can write 1 to 2 sentences rephrasing the topic from the Task 2 introduction information and then state what you are going to write about in the main body.

Examples of what you are going to write about are as follows:

**Discuss both points of view and give your own opinion**
This essay discusses both points of view and then I will give my own opinion.

**Discuss the advantages and disadvantages and give your own opinion**
This essay discusses both advantages and disadvantages and then I will give my own opinion.

An alternative way to answer is –

This essay discusses the advantages and disadvantages of this and then I will give my own perspective on this issue.

**Paragraph 2 – main body**
It is better to have two main points rather than one per main body paragraph. It depends on the task but where possible try to use at least one illustrative example for at least one of the main points. Try to develop each main body paragraph to a similar length.

**Paragraph 3 – main body**
It is better to have two main points rather than one per main body paragraph. It depends on the task but where possible try to use at least one illustrative example for at least one of the main points. Try to develop each main body paragraph to a similar length.

**Paragraph 4 – final paragraph**
It is better to start ALL final paragraphs with – In conclusion – followed by stating:

- both sides of the argument have their merits.
- which side you agree with more strongly and why.

Get your opinion in right at the start of the paragraph as your opinion is one of the three requirements of the question, so you want to say more about it.

If you don't do this then you get grade 5 for Task Response.

# Essay Types - Practice

## Discuss both views and give your own opinion.

Depending on your level of confidence at this point in the book, you can use these practice essays in various ways. You can either use them as simply a reference of this type of essay (and come back to them later and write a complete essay), underline what information you feel is important and needs to be in your essay, write only the introduction or write the whole essay.

**1.**
Many people think cheap air travel should be encouraged because it gives ordinary people freedom to travel further. However, others think it leads to environmental problems and so air travel should be banned.

Discuss both points of view and give your own opinion.

**2.**
Some people believe that governments should help and look after old people, but others believe that people should save money for their lives in their future.

Discuss both points of view and give your own opinion.

**3.**
Some people think that a sense of competition in children should be encouraged. Others believe that children who are taught to cooperate rather than compete become more useful adults.

Discuss both points of view and give your own opinion.

**4.**
Successful sports professionals can earn a great deal more money than people in other important professions. Some people think this is fully justified while others think it is unfair.

Discuss both points of view and give your own opinion.

**5.**
A growing number of people feel that animals should not be exploited by people and that they should have the same rights as humans, while others argue that humans must employ animals to satisfy their various needs, including uses for food and research.

Discuss both points of view and give your own opinion.

**6.**
Some people believe that visitors to other countries should follow local customs and behaviour. Others disagree and think that the host country should welcome cultural differences.

Discuss both points of view and give your own opinion.

# Essay Types - Structures

## Two questions

**Paragraph 1 – introduction**
You can write 1 to 2 sentences rephrasing the topic from the Task 2 introduction information and then state what you are going to write about in the main body.

Examples of how you can express what you are going to write about are as follows:

**Problem / Solution**
This essay discusses the problems associated with this issue and offers possible solutions.

**Cause / Solution**
This essay discusses why this is happening and explores the measures needed to solve this problem.

**Opinion (e.g. Do you agree or disagree?) / Solution**
I agree that financial aid is not the solution to solving the problems in developing countries and will offer possible ways to tackle this issue.

**Discuss the advantages and disadvantages**
**NOTE:** This is best written as a two question essay but could be written as an argument led essay where you discuss both sides and then give your opinion.

**Paragraph 2 – main body**
Now develop your argument in answer to the first Task 2 question.

**Paragraph 3 – main body**
Now develop your argument in answer to the second Task 2 question.

**Paragraph 4 – final paragraph**
It is better to start ALL final paragraphs with – In conclusion – followed by paraphrasing the key points from both main body paragraphs. Avoid using phrases like - As I mentioned before - as this prevents you from showing the examiner that you can paraphrase.

# Essay Types - Practice

# Two Question Essays

Depending on your level of confidence at this point in the book, you can use these practice essays in various ways. You can either use them as simply a reference of this type of essay (and come back to them later and write a complete essay), underline what information you feel is important and needs to be in your essay, write only the introduction or write the whole essay.

**1.**
Nowadays we communicate less with our family members face to face.

What are the causes of this?
What are some potential solutions?

**2.**
In many countries schools have severe problems with student behaviour.

What do you think are the causes of this?
What solutions can you suggest?

**3.**
Alcohol abuse is becoming more and more common in many countries.

What are some of the problems associated with alcohol abuse, and what are some of the possible solutions?

**4.**
Some say it is important for parents to teach their children about the importance of money.

Why and how should they do it?

**5.**
It is often said that the subjects taught in schools are too academic in orientation and that it would be more useful for children to learn about practical matters such as home management, work, and interpersonal skills.

To what extent do you agree?
Which subjects should be taught in school in your opinion?

**6.**
Nowadays, the way many people interact with each other has changed because of technology.

In what ways has technology affected the types of relationships people make?
Has this become a positive or negative development?

# Paragraphs

When thinking about the structure of an essay, a good strategy is to use four paragraphs in total. Some people use more than this but the more paragraphs you use the more your Coherence and Cohesion is likely to suffer. The reason for this is that with more (possibly shorter) paragraphs you have less opportunity to show your skills of cohesion and coherence by linking ideas together within a paragraph.

Taken to an extreme, you will find some students writing a Task 2 essay with only 1-2 sentences in each paragraph. I have even seen students writing in note form and using bullet points to highlight ideas. Expect a very low grade for Coherence and Cohesion if you do this.

What the examiner wants to see is that you can use paragraphs correctly and develop your ideas within the paragraphs in a good flowing manner.

### Introduction – 50 words
You only really need two to three sentences for the introduction.
1. Rephrase the topic.
2. Say what the essay is about or give your opinion for Opinion led essays.

### Main body – 100 words for each of the two main body paragraphs
Develop each main body paragraph according to the type of essay you are writing.

### Final paragraph – 50 words
This is your chance to impress the examiner with your skills in paraphrasing key points from the main body. You will also have to repeat your opinion from the introduction if you are writing an Opinion led essay.

**NOTE:** The minimum number of words needed is 250 words. If you write less than this you will lose one grade from Task Response.

I have suggested an ideal average number of words to use for each paragraph. If you write this exact number of words the total would be 300 words. You can write a little less or a little more but remember that the more you write the less time you have to look for errors and correct them. This will affect your grade for Lexical Resource and Grammatical Range and Accuracy.

**NOTE:** Leave a gap between ALL paragraphs to enable the examiner to see each paragraph more clearly.

# Writing an Introduction

Now that you know more about the structure of each essay type you can begin to develop some ideas for writing the introduction.

**Exercise**
Look at the following introduction examples written by students and decide if the introductions are on topic and written with the correct structure. **An analysis of the three introductions can be found on the next page.**

**A.**
**Some people think that the teenage years are the happiest of our lives, while others believe that adult life brings more happiness.**

**Discuss both these views and give your own opinion**

It is thought by some people that the time of adulthood is the happiest time but others state that adults should have more responsibilities. In my opinion, happiness is vital to the adult but they must be responsible to their family and country.


**B.**
**In most developed countries, the average life expectancy is constantly increasing.**

**Discuss the positive and negative aspects of this trend.**

Longevity in the recent era is nowadays one of the highlighted issues. This is due to the fact that demographic figures have changed tremendously in recent years. While there are numerous advantages of increased life expectancy, it has brought along various problems. This will be proven by analyzing both points of view prior to reaching an informed conclusion.


**C.**
**In many countries, more people than ever before drive private cars.**

**Do you think the advantages of this development outweigh the disadvantages?**

In recent years, it is an obvious fact that there are numerous cars in many countries than there were several decades ago. Having their own car is crucial for people because it makes journeys easier and more comfortable, however, there are also some drawbacks.

# Introduction – Analysis

**A.**
The introduction focuses only on adults and not adults AND teenagers. If this confusion continues into the main body and only information about adults is developed then the Task Response will be grade 5. You MUST talk about both adults and teenagers.

The first sentence suggests that the two opinions are - adulthood is the happiest times - and - adults should have more responsibilities. This does not reflect the two views from the Task 2 information.

The final sentence of the introduction makes it seem like the essay is about your opinion only but you are asked to write about both views and give your opinion. You should write something like, "This essay discusses both points of view and then I will give my own opinion". The opinion then coming in the final paragraph and NOT before.

**B.**
This fails to note that this is about "developed countries" and that life expectancy is "constantly increasing".

The final sentence says that both points of view will be analyzed. However, the instructions ask for the positive and negative aspects of this issue. These should be your opinions. However, an Argument led essay might state, "while some people believe **A** other people feel that **B**". These are view points.

**C.**
It is better to answer the Task 2 question more clearly and directly by stating, for example –

**I am convinced that the advantages of countries having more private cars than before outweigh the disadvantages.**

This then needs to be repeated in the conclusion.

**NOTE:** It is quite common for students to use - overweigh/overweight - instead of - outweigh. These are both wrong and should not be used. Overweigh means to exceed something in weight and - overweight - means you are too fat.

**NOTE:** As you become more familiar with the three main essay types that need to be studied, you will realise that certain basic phrases can be regularly presented in your introduction. If the phrase, we can call it a cohesive phrase, is really good you can use it regularly and it can be written quickly and will always have perfect grammar.

# Introduction - information

To help you avoid the kind of problems we have just seen I would suggest that, before starting to write any of the three essay types, it is essential to look closely at the Task 2 topic information and instructions. I would even suggest reading them 3-4 times so that you notice ALL of the points that are being made. You can even underline the words and phrases that need to be mentioned in your essay.

### Exercise
Look at the Task 2 topics below - A to D - and see if you can notice the different parts of the topic that are important. As we are focusing on the Task 2 topic, the instructions have been left out from the examples. **The answers are at the bottom of this page.**

**A.**
Many governments think that economic progress is their most important goal. Some people, however, think that other types of progress are equally important for a country.

**B.**
Many museums charge for admission while others are free.

**C.**
Some people think that human history has been a journey from ignorance to knowledge. Others argue that this underestimates the achievements of ancient cultures, and overvalues our achievements.

**D.**
Some people think that good health is very important to every person, so medical services should not be run by profit-making companies.

**NOTE:** While the topic information obviously tells you the topic, it also tells you certain aspects of the topic that need to be focused on. Missing any part out and you are heading towards a lower Task Response as a result.

### Answers
**A.**
- many governments / economic progress
- some people / other types of progress / equally important for a country

**B.**
- many museums charge admission
- others are free

**C.**
- some people - human history / a journey from ignorance to knowledge
- this (previous statement) underestimates achievements of ancient cultures/overvalues ours

**D.**
- some people – good health important for everyone / medical services – should not be run by profit-making companies.

# Introduction - information

**Exercise**
Look at the Task 2 topics below - E to I - and see if you can notice the different parts of the topic that are important. As we are focusing on the Task 2 topic, the instructions have been left out from the examples. **The answers are at the bottom of this page.**

**E.**
Some people think that there should be strict laws to control the amount of noise a person makes because of the disturbance it causes to people.

**F.**
Some people believe that competitive sports, both team and individual, have no place in the school curriculum.

**G.**
More and more employees work at home with modern technology. Some people claim that it benefits only workers, but not employers.

**H.**
Some people think that spending a lot on holding wedding parties, birthday parties and other celebrations is just a waste of money. Others, however, think that these are necessary for individuals and the society.

**I.**
Education should be accessible to people of all economic backgrounds. All levels of education, from primary to tertiary education, should be free.

**Answers**
**E.**
- some people - strict laws – control – noise a person makes / causes disturbance to people

**F.**
- some people – competitive sports /team and individual / should not be in school curriculum

**G.**
- more and more employees - work with technology at home / some say this benefits workers not employers.

**H.**
- some people – spending lots on parties / celebrations – waste of money
- others – necessary for individuals / society

**I.**
- education should be available for everyone – all levels of education - free

# Introduction - paraphrasing

You should now be developing some good skills for deciding what parts of the Task 2 information need to be kept and then written about in the essay. As mentioned before, but it is worth repeating, get into the habit of reading the Task 2 information and introduction 3 to 4 times. It is surprisingly easy to overlook something especially if it is not worded like any other essay that you have practiced before.

Another good skill to develop is being able to avoid copying too much from the Task 2 information.

### Exercise
Look at the example written by a student after being given this Task 2 essay:

> **A person's worth nowadays seems to be judged according to social status and material possessions. Old-fashioned values, such as honour, kindness and trust, no longer seem important.**
>
> **To what extent do you agree or disagree with this opinion?**

### Student Example
Someone's worth today is judged according to material possessions and social status. Honour, kindness and trust are old-fashioned values that are no longer important. I totally agree.

### Exercise
What is your opinion of this essay?
What do you like/dislike about it?
How can you improve it?

### Analysis
A few words have been changed, some details deleted, the order changed in places but there is still a huge part of this introduction that has been copied. This is not the way to impress the examiner.

**NOTE**: While these various parts of a topic are very important and help to make your essay complete, try to use different words and phrases as much as possible when writing the introduction. In other words, the examiner is not going to be impressed if most of your introduction is copied from the original.

### Exercise
Try to write a better introduction using the Task 2 essay question above.

# Introduction - paraphrasing

**Exercise**
Look at the Task 2 essay information below (the instructions have not been included) and try to rewrite it using your own words.

> As the number of cars increase, more money has to be spent on road systems. Some people think the government should pay for this. Others, however, think that the users should pay for the cost.

_____
_____
_____
_____
_____
_____

**Analysis**
How similar is your introduction to the original Task 2 introduction?
Have you included all of the important topic points?
Have you been able to paraphrase and use synonyms?

**Exercise**
Now look at the two examples below and decide which one you like best and why.

**Example 1**
   As car numbers continue to increase, it is necessary to spend a lot of money on road infrastructure. One point of view is that funding for this should be paid for by the government. However, others feel that the user should fund this.

**Example 2**
   As more and more people start to use their own car, greater investments need to be made to construct better road infrastructure. While one suggestion is that this should be funded by the government, others state that this is the responsibility of the car user.

# Introduction - examples

While the Task 2 information tells you the topic and the various features of it, the instructions tell you what essay type you should be writing and as a result the structure of the essay.

To understand this more clearly you are going to see some examples of introductions written by students for all three essay types. As you look at each example, look at the Task 2 information and instructions first. Then, read the introduction that the student wrote and make comments about it. These are some questions you can consider:

- Is the introduction too long or too short?
- Has the Task 2 information been paraphrased correctly?
- Are all of the important points from the Task 2 information included?
- Has any information been altered /added that should not be there?
- In Opinion led essays does the last sentence give an opinion?
- In Argument led and Two question essays does the last sentence tell you what the main body is going to be about?

## Which side are you on?

Students often like to sit on the fence of an issue and not have a 100% commitment to an opinion. They do this by using such phrases as – however, nevertheless. Look at the example below:

> **Mixed schools offer a very good way to learn how to cooperate with the opposite sex. However, single-sex schools do, nevertheless, feel more comfortable for many students.**

This style of writing is called concession writing. There is nothing wrong with this style but students have to be careful because if any errors are made with vocabulary or grammar some confusion might result and it might seem as if they have contradicted themselves. This can affect Coherence and Cohesion and Task Response.

Another example of sitting on the fence is when students answer a certain type of Opinion led essay by stating, for example: "I partly agree that students should have a gap year before starting university."

This can go wrong when the student has to argue for both sides of the argument. Remember, they partly agree which means that they partly disagree as well. If the arguments are too strong on one side of the argument the examiner can be left feeling – "Why do they only partly agree?" It seems as if they think this is a really great idea.

**NOTE:** It is MUCH safer and easier to ALWAYS completely agree or disagree.

# Opinion led - introduction examples

**Exercise**
Look at the three essay introductions below (information and instructions) and see if you think they have been written well. Use the questions on the previous page to help you.

**A**

**Arts like music and painting should not be funded by the government.**

**Do you agree or disagree?**

> Many people feel that the government should not invest in arts like music and painting. I agree with this opinion because only a few people benefit from the government's investment, and those who are fond of arts will spend their money voluntarily; however, due to a change in society, government investment in arts is beneficial for a society.

**B.**

**Charities cannot help everyone in the world. They should only provide aid to people in their own communities and countries.**

**Do you agree or disagree?**

> There are numerous charities the world over aiming to support people in need and make a better society. It is argued that an individual charity cannot aid everyone around the globe and should, therefore, focus on helping the needy in their own country. The virtues of this will be shown by looking at the positive effect it has on the amount of people that can be helped and the quality of charity work.

**C.**

**Parents have a definite influence on the development of their children but other influences outside the family play a more important role in children's development.**

**To what extent do you agree or disagree?**

> Fathers and mothers have undeniable effects on how their youngsters develop. However, children are affected more by external factors. I totally agree with this belief because children spend long hours outside their homes and parents have become too busy to look after their kids.

# Opinion led

# Examples analyzed

**A.**

**Arts like music and painting should not be funded by the government.**

**Do you agree or disagree?**

Students have to be careful with concessions (however, nevertheless) as confusion results if you make any errors with vocabulary or grammar. Here the opinion ends up completely confused with the student supporting both sides.

**B.**

**Charities cannot help everyone in the world. They should only provide aid to people in their own communities and countries.**

**Do you agree or disagree?**

This person agrees that charities should only provide aid to people in their own country but hasn't directly answered the question – 'Do you agree or disagree? They could have said – "I agree that helping only your own country is better and the virtues of this will be shown by looking at the positive effect it has on the amount of people that can be helped and the quality of charity work."

**C.**

**Parents have a definite influence on the development of their children but other influences outside the family play a more important role in children's development.**

**To what extent do you agree or disagree?**

Correct!

**NOTE:** The use of the word - **kid** - as a synonym for child is too informal for Task 2 essays.

# Argument led - introduction examples

**A.**
Some say giving to charity helps reduce poverty, whereas others insist it makes the problem worse.

**Discuss both these views and give your opinion.**

It is clear that poverty is a seriously worrying issue and people have different views about finding the effective way of reducing this phenomenon. While many hold the opinion that donations to charities are a good solution to minimise poverty rates, many argue that this way is not effective and instead has had detrimental effects. This essay will highlight both these opinions and then I will propose my own.

**B.**
Some people enjoy keeping pets and treat them as a part of their family. Others feel that this is a waste of money, particularly when there are many people in the world who are starving.

**Discuss both these views and give your opinion.**

A heated controversy has arisen over whether some households should spend a great deal of money and time on pet care or not. While there are some valid arguments to the contrary, I would contend that the considerable expenditure and time needed for taking care of pets should be invested in charities and social activities instead.

**C.**
Some people think that professional athletes make good role models for young people, while others believe they don't.

**Discuss both these points of views and give your own opinion.**

Some people believe that athletes provide useful examples for youngsters but others are of the opinion that this is not the case. In my view there are clear advantages in being a sportsman, and an athlete in particular, however young people can find much better hobbies.

# Argument led

# Examples analyzed

**A.**

**Some say giving to charity helps reduce poverty, whereas others insist it makes the problem worse.**

**Discuss both these views and give your opinion.**

This clearly introduces both points of view and the last sentence states that both points of view will be discussed and then the opinion given (in the conclusion). This type of essay should not have the opinion in the introduction.

**B.**

**Some people enjoy keeping pets and treat them as a part of their family. Others feel that this is a waste of money, particularly when there are many people in the world who are starving.**

**Discuss both these views and give your opinion.**

In contrast to example A. both view points are not clearly given. The fact that one view point states that pet care is a waste of money is not so clear and does not mention the starving people in the world. Also, the opinion has been given in the introduction rather than in the conclusion and it does not state that both view points will be discussed in the way it was in example A.

**C.**

**Some people think that professional athletes make good role models for young people, while others believe they don't.**

**Discuss both these points of views and give your own opinion.**

There are a number of problems here. The topic is about role models but seems to change to useful examples. Also, the opinion has been given in the introduction rather than in the conclusion and refers to hobbies rather than role models.

# Two questions - introduction examples

**A.**
**Nowadays, there are many traffic jams that cause long delays on the roads.**

**Why is this happening?**
**Suggest a solution to the problem.**

Modern life has encountered some pressing problems, one of which is to be stuck in long gridlocks. There are various reasons why this is the case. However, this problem will be alleviated if some prompt measures are taken.

**B.**
**Behaviour in schools is getting worse.**

**Explain the causes and effects of this problem, and suggest some possible solutions.**

It is true that children's behaviour has worsened in schools these days. There are various contributing factors associated with this problem and effective measures need to be taken to address this problem.

**C.**
**In some countries the average weight of people is increasing and their levels of health and fitness are decreasing.**

**What do you think are the causes of these problems and what can be done to solve them?**

It is certainly true that people in developed countries are increasingly overweight nowadays, which has consequently led to a significant decline in the level of people's health. There are several reasons for these issues, and a number of measures can be taken by governments, institutions and individuals to improve the situation. This essay will discuss the root causes of the above mentioned problems and suggest some solutions to them.

# Two questions

# Examples analyzed

**A.**
**Nowadays there are many traffic jams that cause long delays on the roads.**

**Why is this happening?**
**Suggest a solution to the problem.**

This essay introduces the topic and also talks about causes and solutions. It is better, however, to state more clearly that you are going to present a reason for this happening and a solution.


**B.**
**Behaviour in schools is getting worse.**

**Explain the causes and effects of this problem, and suggest some possible solutions.**

The first sentence is rather simple but does introduce the topic. It is better to make it clear that the problem is getting worse (not just worsened). Also, it doesn't state what will be discussed in the main body paragraphs. Note that this particular essay is asking the student to discuss the causes, effects, and problems (three things in total). Usually, only two things will be asked for – causes/solutions or effects/solutions.


**C.**
**In some countries the average weight of people is increasing and their levels of health and fitness are decreasing.**

**What do you think are the causes of these problems and what can be done to solve them?**

This does offer some good background information to the topic but it changes the focus from "some countries" to "developed countries". Also, there is no need for both of the last two sentences. They both talk about causes and solutions. The last sentence is better.

# Getting Ready to Write

You do not know everything you need to know to write an excellent essay, but it is a good idea to look at the different steps you can follow to help streamline the writing process.

The more you are in control of the writing process, the easier (and quicker) it is to write a good essay without forgetting something important and so lowering your grade.

## 10 simple steps to help you improve

1. Pick a Task 2 question to write.

2. Start the timer for 40 minutes.

3. Read the topic information and instructions.

4. Read the topic information again and underline all the words that you think must be part of the introduction.

5. Read the instructions again and decide which of the three main essay types it is.

6. Make a note of the structure that you need.

7. Make notes of your main ideas for the two main body paragraphs.

8. As you write, try to make sure that the two main body paragraphs are a similar length.

9. Make sure that the conclusion is developed enough - about 45 to 50 words.

10. After finishing, quickly proofread for grammatical and vocabulary errors and see how long it took to write.

# Task 2 – Writing Practice - 1

Here is the first of a number of Task 2 questions to practice writing that you will find in this book. Use the ideas and knowledge that you have gained so far to write this essay and use the space below to develop your ideas. Write your essays on a separate piece of paper.

**Some people think that the teenage years are the happiest of our lives, while others believe that adult life brings more happiness.**

**Discuss both these views and give your own opinion**

# Task 2 – Writing Practice - 2

Some people think that elderly people should be forced to retire at a certain age, such as 65. Others say that people should be allowed to work for as long as they are able and want to.

Discuss both sides of this argument and then give your own opinion.

# PART II

# Brainstorming

Students are often recommended, before starting to write an essay, to spend a few minutes brainstorming for ideas.

Brainstorming is an excellent idea but this really only works if the ideas are somewhere in your brain to come out when thinking about them! If you have never had these ideas then, no matter how long you brainstorm for, no ideas will come.

**Developing ideas**
You might now ask how you put the ideas in your brain in the first place. This sounds as if it could take a long time as there are many different topics that could be used to develop Task 2 essays.

These ideas come through practical experience, travelling, conversations, reading, watching movies, documentaries and the like, listening to the radio and so on. Any of these take time – often a long time – and sometimes lots of money! Luckily, there is a quick way to get these 'experiences'.

**Topics**
Typical Task 2 essay topics are shown in the table below.

| Culture | Economy | Global Village | Television |
|---|---|---|---|
| Education | Transport | Work | Salaries |
| Technology | Communication | Lifestyle | Languages |
| Society | Health | Food | Art |
| Environment | Fitness | Computers | Music |

**A much longer list is provided on pages 4 - 7.**

# Brainstorming by Googling

Googling helps you – by using only a few words – to get great ideas in only a few minutes. Now, you can not do this in the exam but this is a fantastic way to prepare for the exam. Take as many Task 2 topics as you can and try this quick and easy way to develop ideas.

## How to Google

Some of these topics are more specific than others and so, perhaps, easier to research online for ideas. If we Google – coeducation - we end up with nearly 2 million hits and if we Google – advantages disadvantages coeducation – you get just over 2 million hits.

This is, nevertheless, a lot of hits but by looking at no more than the first ten listed sites you will usually find lists of both the advantages and disadvantages.

You don not need all of the advantages and disadvantages listed on one site. Usually, those listed nearer the beginning of the list are more important so look at these first. When you have a few ideas you can even practice writing a few sentences incorporating these new ideas and new vocabulary that you will also get by looking at the list.

By doing this for a range of topics you will develop your ability to think of good ideas quickly as well as increase your vocabulary range. This is good for your – Task Response – and your – Lexical Resource.

## Analysis

By only Googling - advantages disadvantages coeducation - the following ideas were obtained:

### Advantages of a coeducation system

- Mutual understanding between sexes
- Increased confidence levels
- Develops a broader mind
- Environment similar to a real society
- Helps to defeat sexist attitudes

### Disadvantages of a coeducation system

- Low concentration
- Unethical activities
- More social pressure from both sexes

However, you might be thinking – How does this help me when I am trying to develop ideas for essays that are not advantage and disadvantage essays? We will look at this on the next page.

# Brainstorming by Googling

Let's look at each essay type and see how Googling for ideas can help. Each essay type has one set of instructions that ask about the advantages and disadvantages of something so Googling is perfect for these as you have already seen.

**Opinion led**
- Do you agree or disagree?
- What is your opinion?
- **Do the advantages outweigh the disadvantages?**
- To what extent do you agree or disagree?

**NOTE:** To explain why you agree or disagree (or the extent you agree or disagree) you can offer the advantages / disadvantages of the topic as reasons why you have this opinion. Your opinion can often be based on the advantages / disadvantages of something.

**Argument led**
- **Discuss the advantages and disadvantages and give your own opinion**
- Discuss both points of view and give your own opinion

**NOTE:** Why people have a certain point of view is usually because they think of something in a favourable or positive way. These are the advantages.

**Two questions**
- Problem / Solution
- Cause / Solution
- **Discuss the advantages and disadvantages**
- Opinion (e.g. Do you agree or disagree?) / Solution

**NOTE:** This is the hardest of the three essay types to find ideas from Googling. This will, however, work for two of these essays:

- **Discuss the advantages and disadvantages**
- Opinion (e.g. Do you agree or disagree?) / Solution

The other two essays can be Googled using the key words from the essay introduction. For both essays it is very easy to Google for a solution.

**For example:**
Problem / Solution
**You can Google** for – solution "traffic congestion"

Cause / Solution
**You can Google for** – solution "endangered species"

Hopefully, your knowledge is sufficient to able to help with the first part of each of the questions – **problem** and **cause**.

# Task 2 – Writing Practice - 3

Some people think that computer games are bad for children, while others believe that they are useful.

Discuss the advantages and disadvantages of computer games and give your own opinion.

# Task 2 – Writing Practice - 4

In most developed countries, the average life expectancy is constantly increasing.

Discuss the positive and negative aspects of this trend.

# Cohesive Phrases

Understanding what cohesive phrases are and learning to use them effectively will not only help increase your grade for Coherence and Cohesion but will also help improve your Lexical Resource and Grammatical Range and Accuracy. Knowing this should encourage you to develop good cohesive phrases that help to strengthen the structure of the essays that you are writing.

These phrases, it is possible to use several in each essay, will also help you write your essay more quickly. Imagine having 50 words in your essay that you have already prepared – perfect grammar, perfect spelling, perfect cohesion – all waiting to be written!

Cohesive phrases can be as simple as using a word like – **and** – to a much longer phrase like – **There has been an ongoing discussion for many years about … …**

All of them, however, act to link together ideas within a sentence, between sentences, and between paragraphs. They not only let ideas flow more smoothly but also help lift your level of writing to a better grade.

Cohesive phrases, once you learn how to use them, can be used to help form a structure within your writing that allows you to write the essay more quickly because you already have a collection of phrases that you can use for all three essay types.

**Common Phrases**
While you will see a lot of cohesive phrases later in this book, let's start with a few of the more basic ones:

**Addition Transitions**
and, also, besides, in addition, furthermore, moreover, to begin with, next, finally

**Cause-Effect Transitions**
accordingly, and so, as a result, consequently, for this reason, hence, so, then, therefore, thus

**Comparison Transitions**
by the same token, in like manner, in the same way, in similar fashion, likewise, similarly

**Contrast Transitions**
but, however, in contrast, instead, nevertheless, on the contrary, on the other hand, still, yet

**Example Transitions**
as an example, for example, for instance, specifically, thus, to illustrate

**Insistence Transitions**
in fact, indeed

**Restatement Transitions**
in other words, in short, in simpler terms, that is, to put it differently, to repeat

# Cohesive Phrases

By studying the rest of this book you will know what type of ideas need to be presented in your essays and you will be able to develop a much better framework on which to develop your essays.

Good phrases will help to position each main body paragraph into a suitable direction to add appropriate ideas and examples. They will also help to make it very clear to the examiner what your opinion is.

**For example:**

- The primary reason why ……
- By far the most important point to highlight is that there ……
- One of the main causes of ……
- One major problem caused by ……
- The most important factor needed to help is ……
- In order to achieve these goals ……
- We can address this issue by ……
- This policy if implemented would be able to make significant inroads into reducing this problem.
- The primary reason why I completely agree/disagree is because ……
- Another reason I completely agree/disagree is because ……

# Introduction

When writing an introduction, certain phrases will let you start your essay with a more academic style and help you introduce the topic more easily.

**Exercise**
Before you continue, can you think of any ways to start an introduction? Try to write a few ideas down.

_____

_____

_____

Now look at a few examples and see how they are quite general in content but at the same time flexible in how they can be used. Try looking at a few Task 2 introductions and then try to use one or more of these phrases to help you introduce the topic.

♦ There has been an ongoing discussion for many years about …… (**add Task 2 topic**)

♦ While some people think that ……, others are of the opinion that ……

♦ Nowadays, improving …… (**add Task 2 topic**) …… is one of the most controversial issues of our time.

♦ One of the most controversial issues today relates to …… (**add Task 2 topic**)

The examiner is always looking for signs of an ability to write in a cohesive manner. So, if you tend to write mainly with short sentences start linking some sentences together.

**Exercise**
With this in mind, look at part of an introduction and see if you can think of how you can make it more cohesive.

**Longevity in the modern era is often discussed. This is due to the fact that demographic figures have changed tremendously in recent years.**

**Analysis**
In the introduction it would have been better if the first two sentences had been combined. This is done by changing the order of the sentences. This would change to:

**Due to the fact that demographic figures have changed tremendously in the modern era, longevity is now often discussed.**

# Introduction

**Exercise**
Look at the Two question essay below and note the key information and instructions.

> **Alcohol abuse is becoming more and more common in many countries.**
>
> **What are some of the problems associated with alcohol abuse, and what are some of the possible solutions?**

**Exercise**
Now look at the two sample introductions written by students that follow. Which one do you think is better and why?

**A.**
The issue of alcohol addiction is more prevalent in the world. The age of people who have alcohol addiction has become lower. This essay will discuss the effect of alcohol abuse on society and communities, and offer some solutions from the government to its citizens.

**B.**
Drinking too much is tending to become a prevalent problem in many communities; however, it is obvious that it threatens many societies. Its effects can also be tackled successfully. This essay looks at some of the problems caused by alcohol abuse on society, and suggests some solutions to reduce the effects.

**Analysis**
The first example does not have a lot of cohesion but does work. It also explains what will be discussed in the main body paragraphs. The second example is a little more cohesive and also states what will be discussed in the main body paragraphs.

**Exercise**
Why do you think the first example is less cohesive?

**Analysis**
The reason the first example is less cohesive is because the first two sentences are quite short – 11 words each. This has the effect of making what we read seem jerky or less cohesive because we are having to stop and start between sentences more often than with slightly longer – more cohesive – sentences. However, try not to make your sentence too long as this can, depending on your grammar skills, lead to too many grammar errors. Sentences that are 20 to 30 words in length are ideal.

# Introduction

To develop good cohesive phrases for the introduction you need to consider the essay type you are writing and what kind of information you are trying to link with the cohesive phrase.

## Exercise
Look at the table below with ten cohesive phrases. Imagine where they might go in an essay - introduction, main body, or conclusion.

| with this in mind | for example |
|---|---|
| many scholars are now convinced that | all in all, I am firmly convinced |
| another way to help address this problem would be if | the first recommendation would be to provide |
| in addition | finally |
| this essay first looks at possible problems of this phenomenon and then offers | therefore |

## Exercise
Now, read the Task 2 essay information and instructions and try to match the correct cohesive phrases from the table above with the appropriate places – 1, 2 or 3 – in the introduction below.

### Task 2
A rapidly increasing global population will lead to many social and environmental problems unless something is done to help control this impending catastrophe.

What are some of these social and environmental problems?
Suggest ways to help slow down this trend.

### Introduction

1........................ future wars will be triggered by a lack of land, food and water rather than for political reasons. One of the main causes of this is likely to be the global population explosion. It is **2.** ......................... essential that ways to help control this are put into action before it is too late. **3.** ......................... several suggestions to help make inroads into this problem.

**Look at page 78 in the ANSWER section at the back of this book.**

# Introduction

# Time

Most of the topics discussed in IELTS Task 2 essays are current issues rather than topics that are part of history and this point needs to be expressed in the introduction.

This is something students sometimes have difficulty with and so a few ideas will be given here to help speed up your understanding of how you can do this. The time related phrases are presented in **bold** and other phrases that can help build up your collection of ideas of useful cohesive phrases are underlined.

- **Nowadays**, improving public health is one of the most controversial issues of our time.

- **Nowadays, a lot of people tend to** move to another country to either study or work.

- **One of the most controversial issues today** relates to the age when people should retire.

- **In today's modern world, there is no doubt that** sporting and artistic events have become lucrative businesses for many people.

- It has been commonly observed that involvement in criminal activities by youngsters has increased tremendously **over the last few decades**.

- There is no doubt that technological advances, **in recent years,** have increasingly led to an availability of items such as mobile phones and personal computers.

- **In today's interconnected world,** there are many opportunities to travel and learn about cultures all over the globe.

- **It is not uncommon these days** for some people to like working in teams, while others prefer working independently.

- **In recent years**, due to rising juvenile delinquency, many people feel that schools should teach morals while others feel that this is unnecessary.

- **In this information era**, newspapers play a big part in shaping people's thoughts and are a main source of information.

**NOTE:** Try to commit the phrases you like to memory and start to use them with the many Task 2 practice tasks given to you in this book. You can even go back to essays you have already written (or simply studied) and see if you can improve them by adding better cohesive phrases.

# Task 2 – Writing Practice - 5

Some people think students at schools and universities learn far more from lessons with teachers than from others sources (such as the internet and television).

Do you agree or disagree?

# Task 2 – Writing Practice - 6

Some people believe that museums and art galleries are not essential for a society and they should not be funded by the government. Others, however, believe that support from the government should be provided.

Discuss both these views and give your own opinion.

# Main Body

As you become more familiar with the three main essay types that need to be studied you will realise that certain basic phrases can also be regularly presented in your main body.

**Exercise**
Look at the example of the Task 2 information and instructions asking about whether or not students learn more from teachers or from electronic devices.

> **Computers are being used more and more in education and so there will soon be no role for the teacher in education.**
>
> **To what extent do you agree or disagree?**

**Exercise**
Now look at the first sentence of paragraphs two and three for this essay and pay particular attention to the phrases in bold.

> **Firstly,** students can learn from materials and devices at any time and in any place.
>
> **Secondly,** using these sources makes it possible for governments or schools to offer several levels of education and many resources.

**Exercise**
What do you think about these phrases? Would you use them in your essays? Why? Why not?

**Analysis**
We can certainly say that these phrases work and are similar to a number of phrases that could also be used in the same way:

firstly / secondly
first / second
first of all / second of all

However, these phrases are rather lacking in substance. They are rather simple and prevent you from showing the examiner something better. "Is this all this student can think of writing?" the examiner might say to himself. You are meant to be trying to impress him.

The secret of course is to develop better phrases for all of the different types of information you might need to present in your essays.

**Example**
Look at how better cohesive phrases are used here.

> **The most important point is that** students can learn from materials and devices at any time and in any place.
>
> **In addition to this,** using these sources makes it possible for governments or schools to offer several levels of education and many resources.

# Main Body

Let us look a little more closely at some useful cohesive phrases for some of the different essay types you should practice.

## Opinion led

When thinking of good cohesive phrases for the agree/disagree essays it is a good idea to use the following phrases for the start of the two main body paragraphs.

**Do you agree or disagree with this statement?**

- The main reason why I agree/disagree is because
- Another reason I agree/disagree is because

**To what extent do you agree or disagree with this statement?**

- The main reason why I completely agree/disagree is because
- Another reason I completely agree/disagree is because

**NOTE:** These phrases, as part of the topic sentence for each paragraph, explain very simply but clearly that the paragraphs that follow will explain why you have a particular opinion. In other words, we know why we are reading the two main body paragraphs

## Argument led

When writing a - Discuss both these views and give your own opinion. - you could use the following phrases.

- Some people are convinced that
- There are, however, strong arguments against this claim because

## Two questions

The following phrases are excellent for a typical problem / solution essay.

- One undeniable problem caused by
- One way to help address this issue would be for the government to impose

# Topic Sentence

Make sure that the two main body paragraphs have a topic sentence as the first sentence. You need to make each topic sentence general enough to express the main idea of the paragraph rather than just one detail but specific enough to allow the examiner to know what the focus of the paragraph is.

On reading the rest of the paragraph you should be able to see that it is developing or explaining the topic sentence in more detail. If this is not the case, then the paragraph has not done justice to the topic sentence and needs to be rewritten.

Four possible situations should be looked for:

- a good topic sentence / a good paragraph
- a good topic sentence / a bad paragraph
- a bad topic sentence / a good paragraph
- a bad topic sentence / a bad paragraph

These situations are getting progressively worse and need a lot of rewriting to make them acceptable for a Task 2 IELTS essay.

**Exercise**
Read the Task 2 information and instructions and the example paragraph below (written by a student). Decide if the topic sentence is well written. Make comments if needed.

> **Some people say that what children watch on TV influences their behaviour, while others say the amount of time children spend watching TV influences their behaviour.**
>
> **Discuss both views and give your opinion.**

On the one hand, it is undeniable that constantly being exposed to certain TV programs does have a psychological effect on a baby's development. For example, my 10-year-old nephew who used to watch violent scenes on news programs a lot had to go to a psychologist after aggressively bullying two of his friends in school. This may be explained by the fact that children's brains are not fully developed and, therefore, cannot distinguish right from wrong. They often imitate adults behaviour with a thought that those ways of behaving are good without thinking of the severe consequences.

**Read the analysis of this on the next page.**

# Topic Sentence

**Analysis**

The topic sentence on the previous page refers to babies and not children. It is, therefore, off topic.

The examiner not only looks for the way you have used a cohesive phrase to introduce the rest of the topic sentence but to see if the topic sentence is accurate. Did you really focus on this topic in the rest of the paragraph? is a question you should really ask yourself.

Also, even if you have focused on the correct point being discussed - have you used good Lexical Resource and Grammatical Range and Accuracy?

**Exercise**

Look at the Task 2 information and instructions below and start to think how you might introduce the two main body paragraphs. What cohesive phrases do you think you could use?

> **Some people believe that museums and art galleries are not essential for a society and they should not be funded by the government.**
>
> **What is your opinion?**

**Exercise**

Look at the two main body paragraphs written by a student for the essay information and instructions shown above.

**Paragraph 2**

> The main reason why I believe museums and art galleries are compulsory for a community and the government should support them financially is that these places provide people with intellectual achievements. Museums and art galleries demonstrate the ways of living and the types of traditions in the past. For example, citizens become aware of the culture of past generations by looking at their pictures and watching the documentaries related to them in museums.

**Paragraph 3**

> In addition people connect with each other regarding what they see and read in museums and art galleries. Consequently, they will be able to share their thoughts and opinions about the displayed pictures and videos there. This helps citizens to enjoy their free time, to build strong relationships and to create the neighbourhood together.

**Exercise**

Try to decide if the topic sentences need changing. If so, how would you change them and why?

**Read an analysis of the two paragraphs shown here on the next page.**

# Topic Sentence

**Analysis**

Let's look at the two main body paragraphs again to see how the topic sentence can be changed.

**Paragraph 2**

> The main reason why I believe museums and art galleries are compulsory for a community and the government should support them financially is that these places provide people with intellectual achievements. Museums and art galleries demonstrate the ways of living and the types of traditions in the past. For example citizens become aware of the culture of past generations by looking at their pictures and watching the documentaries related to them in museums.

**Revised Topic Sentence**

> **The main reason why I believe museums and art galleries are important is because of their educational value.**

The revised topic sentence is more concise and shows that the focus should be on the educational value of museums and art galleries and not intellectual achievements or finances.

**Paragraph 3**

> In addition people connect with each other regarding what they see and read in museums and art galleries. Consequently, they will be able to share their thoughts and opinions about the displayed pictures and videos there. This helps citizens to enjoy their free time, to build strong relationships and to create the neighbourhood together.

**Revised Topic Sentence**

> **In addition, museums have social value for a community.**

The revised topic sentence is more concise and shows that the focus is on connecting with other people. This has been expressed more clearly by stating that museums and art galleries offer social value to the community.

# Essay Analysis

One very good way of improving your writing style is to look at as many essays as you can that have been written by students. You can find many of them online.

If an assessment of an essay has already been made – ignore it. For one thing, we often do not know how experienced the person is who critiqued the essay but the main point here is that YOU should be the examiner looking for issues of one kind or another.

**Exercise**

Use the checklist below and on the next page to help you when you are analyzing essays..

## 1. Errors in Task 2 information

_____
_____
_____
_____
_____

## 2. Errors in Task 2 instructions

_____
_____
_____
_____
_____

## 3. Errors in following essay type structure

_____
_____
_____
_____
_____

# Essay Analysis

4. Are cohesive phrases used correctly?
_____
_____
_____
_____
_____

5. Are the topic sentences well written?
_____
_____
_____

6. Use the tables below to list any errors for grammar and vocabulary. Then correct these errors in the tables.

| Grammar ||
|---|---|
| Errors | Corrected |
|  |  |
|  |  |
|  |  |
|  |  |
|  |  |
|  |  |

| Vocabulary ||
|---|---|
| Errors | Corrected |
|  |  |
|  |  |
|  |  |
|  |  |
|  |  |
|  |  |

# Essay Analysis

**Exercise**
Read the Task 2 information and instructions and then read the essay below. Use the check list on the previous two pages to help you analyze this carefully. Make notes if you need to.

**Many young people nowadays graduate from schools with a negative attitude.**

**Why do you think this happens?**
**What can be done to solve or reduce this problem?**


The social media has been paying particular attention in recent years to a disturbing phenomena of a negative attitude in many students graduating form university. The purpose of this essay is to looking at some of the causes of negativity in school graduates.

It is difficult to refuse the fact that social media in all its guises has contribute to students feeling rather pesimistic about their future. When students are constantly bombarded with information about natural resources running out, environmental pollution, war in different countries around the world and high unemployment, it is, perhaps, understandable if after hearing all of these negatives that students pick up on this and also feel negative about life.

We can start to alter this issue by students exposing to more optimistic view of the university. This can be done by instilling into each student the belief that they are in charge of their destiny regardless of what is happens in the world. This can also be achieved by focusing on role models who have made a success of their lives despite coming from humble beginnings and having seemingly impossible hurdle to cross before they could have success.

In summary, with access to more media than in any previous generation students are constantly surrounded by positive views of the world and by reflection their future. To balance this schools need to present what appears to be taboo to presenters of daily news and that is good news. Having guest lecturers at the school, showing motivational movies and using inspirational books as reading projects will help students see that life is a mix of good and bad and will help ensure they remain motivated after graduating.

# Essay Analysis

### 1. Errors in Task 2 information

**The** social media **has been paying particular attention in recent years to a disturbing phenomena of** a negative attitude in many students graduating form university.

✓ You should be focusing on schools NOT universities.

**In conclusion,** with access to more media than in any previous generation students are constantly surrounded by positive views of the world and by reflection their future.

✓ You should have put - negative views of the world.

### 2. Errors in Task 2 instructions

You did not mention that you are going to offer a solution. You could write: **The purpose of this essay is to look at some of the causes of negativity in school graduates as well as offer a practical solution to this.**

### 3. Errors in following essay type structure

✓ This has been done successfully.

### 4. Are cohesive phrases used correctly?

**We can start to alter this issue by** students exposing to more optimistic view of the world.

✓ You should have said - **We can start to address this issue by**

**In summary,**

✓ You need to write - **In conclusion,** - for ALL Task essays.

### 5. Are the topic sentences well written?

**We can start to alter this issue by** students exposing to more optimistic view of the university.

✓ It makes a lot more sense to write - more optimistic view of the world.

# Essay Analysis

6. Grammar and vocabulary.

| Grammar | |
|---|---|
| Errors | Corrected |
| is to looking at some | is to look at some |
| has contribute | has contributed |
| war in different countries | wars in different countries |
| students exposing | exposing students / students being exposed |
| to more optimistic view | to a more optimistic view |
| to balance this schools | to balance this, schools |

| Vocabulary | |
|---|---|
| Errors | Corrected |
| phenomena | phenomenon |
| form | from |
| refuse | refute |
| pesimistic | pessimistic |
| happens | happening / regardless of what happens |
| hurdle | hurdles |

Look at page 79 to see grammar and vocabulary errors underlined in text.

# Task 2 – Writing Practice - 7

Recycling is now an essential measure: it is time for everyone in society to become more responsible towards the environment.

To what extent do you agree or disagree with this statement?

# Task 2 – Writing Practice - 8

In many countries, more people than ever before drive private cars.

Do you think the advantages of this development outweigh the disadvantages?

# Expressing Positive / Negative Effects

Many of the issues you have to deal with are situations that are getting worse:

- more and more rubbish is being produced
- noise pollution is becoming a bigger and bigger problem
- fitness levels are decreasing all the time

**NOTE:** When writing about many of these issues you must make it clear that the issue is becoming - **more and more** - of a problem. Simply stating for the examples shown above that, for example, a lot of rubbish is being produced, there is a lot of noise pollution or fitness levels have fallen is not correct.

There are, nevertheless, times when you need to express the idea of positivity or that certain facts are indeed true (even if these facts are negative) Take, for example, the following cohesive phrases: The phrases are highlighted in bold.

**There is no denying that / There is no doubt that / It is undeniable that / It is quite evident that**

These can be used in a positive or negative way depending on what comes after the cohesive phrases:

- **There is no denying that** technology has paved the way for the proliferation of many profitable online businesses.

- **It is quite evident that** obesity can no longer be classed as a problem exclusive to adults.

**Exercise**
Study the list of cohesive phrases that follows and then try to incorporate some of these ideas into your writing.

**One obvious benefit is that** businesses can execute deals or finish transactions online as an alternative to a lengthy commute.

**This is an unarguable contribution of** technology when people can now easily get acquainted with others and share information with one another.

**It is also possible to say that** living in another country makes one more broad-minded as he or she learns about that country's cultural nuances.

**This trend also has a significant effect on** society as a whole.

# Solutions

As you now know, writing about solutions can be an important part of a Two question essay.

Being able to present your solutions in a more developed style is important if you are going to impress the examiner.

Many students simply write something like:

- ♦ The government **should** introduce stronger laws.
- ♦ Parents **need to** closely monitor the activities of their children.
- ♦ Companies **must** develop cleaner production systems.

**NOTE:** Very often solutions are introduced by using - **should, need to, must** as seen above. However, while these ideas do allow various solutions to be presented, there are many better ways to present them. The phrases are highlighted in bold.

**To eradicate the difference between** the rich and poor, governments and international organizations have a huge responsibility on their hands.

**Simply providing** money or food to underprivileged people will not result in any long-term success.

**The most important thing is to help people** establish the correct concepts regarding a balanced diet.

**In order to achieve those goals,** the government can begin to develop a better public transport system to encourage people to leave their car at home in favour of buses or MRT.

**Various other approaches exist that if implemented would have a significant effect on** reducing industrial emissions.

**However, despite the vital role of** governments, **we should not ignore the important effect of** people **in minimising such damage.**

**We have no alternative but to take immediate steps to address this situation by** providing incentives for local business (restaurants, supermarkets and shops) to use recycled materials.

**We can address this issue by** gradually increasing the price of alcohol so that sales will be reduced.

# Cause and Effects

Another common feature of a Two question essay is having to write about the causes and effects of a problem. Look at a few examples written by students for both causes and effects. The phrases are highlighted in bold.

**Cause - the reason why something (a problem) has happened**

**The main cause of this problem** is poor diet

**The foremost causes of** obesity are an inactive lifestyle and unhealthy eating habits.

**Moreover, the problem is accentuated by the growing number of people**, who eat irregularly and consume large portions of high-calorie food.

**One of the most important causes giving rise to this problem** is the amount of time people now spend at work.

**Effects - the result (the problem) of something happening**

**The possible effects of this problem include** physical health problems and loss of productivity.

Today more and more people rely on cars instead of walking, have less physical demands at work and prefer inactive leisure activities. **This results in** burning less calories and gaining weight.

Secondly, overweight people are very unhealthy and **often suffer from** stress and tiredness. **This lessens their** work capacity and **results in** lower productivity.

**One of the notable consequences of** an ageing community is the need for extra medical facilities.

The noticeable increase in children becoming overweight **may lead to problems with** low self esteem

# Conclusion

If we think more carefully about the purpose of having a conclusion, it becomes easier and quicker to write.

ALL conclusions offer the examiner the opportunity to see if you can select the key points of importance from the main body and then paraphrase them in a concise manner. If you can do this without copying long phrases from the main body then you have a great skill that will help you get a higher grade for Coherence and Cohesion and Task Response.

Other reasons for having a conclusion are based on the essay type that you are writing.

## Opinion led

- you need to repeat the opinion that you presented in the introduction (the answer to the Task 2 question).
- present key points from the main body for the side you favour
- when agreeing or disagreeing you can give a final opinion or recommendation.

## Argument led

- state that both sides of the argument have their merits.
- state which side you agree with more strongly and why.
- get your opinion in right at the start of the paragraph as your opinion is one of the three requirements of the question, so you want to say more about it.

## Two question

- present key points form BOTH main body paragraphs.

**NOTE:** There are various ways to start the final paragraph but the simplest way is by writing:- In conclusion. It is better to avoid the more informal (or clichéd) ways like – In a nutshell / All in all - as these have been used many times by students and never fail to make the examiner groan!

# Task 2 – Writing Practice - 9

The world is experiencing a dramatic increase in population. This is causing problems not only for poor, undeveloped countries, but also for industrialised and developing nations.

Describe some of the problems that overpopulation causes, and suggest at least one possible solution.

# Task 2 – Writing Practice - 10

Some people feel that certain workers like nurses, doctors and teachers are undervalued and should be paid more, especially when other people like film actors and company bosses are paid huge sums of money that are out of proportion to the importance of the work that they do.

How far do you agree?
What criteria should be used to decide how much people are paid?

# Task 2 – Writing Practice - 1

## Model Answer - 1

Some people think that the teenage years are the happiest of our lives, while others believe that adult life brings happiness.

Discuss both these views and give your own opinion

**There is no doubt that changes in** value systems in many countries **in recent years** have increasingly led to a freer world for the younger generations to explore their interests. **As a result,** sociologists often wonder if the happiest years of our lives are in our teens rather than in adult life. **In this essay I am going to examine this question from both points of view and then give my own opinion on the matter.**

**One obvious benefit** of being a teenager **is that**, apart from the need to do well in your studies, there are no other responsibilities. **This means that** you can spend your free time with your friends and enjoy life as much as possible. The summer holidays, in particular, can be a time for travelling and indulging yourself in your hobbies and interests while at the same experiencing so many new things. The key to having fun as a teenager is knowing that you have lots of free time and a thirst for trying new and ever more exciting things.

**There is no denying, however, that** adults have the advantage when it comes to having more disposable income and not having to ask permission to do anything. Certain places, like pubs and clubs, once restricted because of age, are now available and problems in getting to certain places through not having personal transport have disappeared. Although adults often have a lot more responsibilities than teenagers, this is often more than compensated for by knowing from past experience what you really enjoy and having the means to indulge in these activities.

**In conclusion, I believe both sides of the argument have their merits. On balance, however, I tend to believe that** given a reasonable income adulthood is more likely to be happier than the teen years because as an adult you can focus on the things you really enjoy and spend your money and time doing the things that make you the happiest

# Task 2 – Writing Practice - 2

## Model Answer - 2

Some people think that elderly people should be forced to retire at a certain age, such as 65. Others say that people should be allowed to work for as long as they are able and want to.

Discuss both sides of this argument and then give your own opinion.

As more and more people are living longer, when to retire **has become a major issue.** Some people feel that a certain age should be stated by the government as the time to retire while others suggest leaving the decision to the person working. **In this essay I am going to examine this question from both points of view and then give my own opinion on the matter.**

**Some people contend that one of the main causes of** unemployment in the young is the extended working life of older people. If government legislation made it a legal necessity to retire at, for example, 65 years of age, then younger people would be able take their first step into the business world more easily and more quickly than at present. It is, perhaps, a given that younger people are the future of our economic growth and possess more passion and willingness to learn than people in their 60s who now work too slowly for a fast-paced society.

**There are, however, strong arguments against this claim because** experience and ability gained over years and years in the corporate world should not be thrown onto the scrap heap with such impunity. While older workers may well work more slowly than a younger employee they are likely to work more efficiently and be more selective in terms of how they spend their time. One must also consider who would train the new business minds if the older workers are being retired. As these veterans of the company are responsible for its success no one is more qualified to mould the latest talents into successful businessmen in the future.

**In conclusion, I believe both sides of the argument have their merits. On balance, however, I tend to believe that a middle ground approach would be more effective than adopting one side or the other.** It is certainly true that the older employees are the backbone of the company and can offer knowledge, experience and training opportunities for new employees and should, therefore, be kept on as long as possible. However, if someone prefers to retire earlier than the standard retirement age due either to health issues or simply wanting to have more free time then they should be allowed to do so.

# Task 2 – Writing Practice - 3

## Model Answer - 3

Some people think that computer games are bad for children, while others believe that they are useful.

Discuss the advantages and disadvantages of computer games and give your own opinion.

**It is, perhaps, inevitable that** with the rapid spread of computer games throughout our society many people now consider their effects to be harmful on the children that play them. Others, however, deem them as clearly useful and an important part of a child's development. **In this essay I am going to examine this question from both points of view and then give my own opinion on the matter.**

**By far the most important positive point to highlight is that** computer games offer children an escape from the pressures of studying. This is an excellent way to forget about the need to get high grades in every test and enter the world of video games. Here, they can forge friendships with other gamers and become more computer savvy especially in terms of eye-hand coordination and problem solving.

**By contrast**, other people feel that computer games are highly addictive and so, apart from the physical harm done by playing games for a long period of time such as eye strain, wrist injuries and postural problems, they create a false world where children lose interest in studying and start to mix with unsavoury people or shrink into their own world and never mix socially with their peers.

**In conclusion, I believe both sides of the argument have their merits. On balance, however, I tend to believe that** computer games, if used moderately, are of great benefit to children. They do allow children a way to relax after a day spent studying at school and they also help develop good hand-eye coordination and a competitive spirit that is so important in both the academic and corporate world.

# Task 2 – Writing Practice - 4

## Model Answer - 4

In most developed countries, the average life expectancy is constantly increasing.

Discuss the positive and negative aspects of this trend.

The constantly increasing life expectancy in many developed countries around the world **has become a major talking point in social media for sometime. While this is seen by many as of great benefit to both the individual and society, others feel that this trend presents many problems. In this essay I am going to examine the positive and negative aspects of this global situation.**

**One obvious benefit of** living longer for the individual is simply in providing more time to enjoy life especially after retirement. The things we all wanted to do when we were working, our bucket lists, can now be achieved because we have more free time. **In terms of society**, a wealth of knowledge and experience gained by many people can remain an active part of society, in business and in life itself, giving us a chance to learn more about our culture, history and skills needed to develop our careers.

**The negative aspects of** a longer life is that we need to consider how these people, as they become less and less active, are going to be cared for. Many of these people are likely to have either no children or only one making it difficult or impossible to be looked after by their offspring. **This places the burden firmly in the hands of the government** who then needs to find the necessary resources and funding to make this possible. Somewhere in this equation is almost certainly an increase in tax for everyone who works.

**In conclusion, I tend to believe that** as this is an inevitable trend that will include more and more countries in the future, we need to focus on the positive aspects of being old such as more leisure time and having the opportunity to continue your career if so desired. The government must also face the reality of having to fund the necessary resources to help the elderly who are less physically active and less financially secure.

# Task 2 – Writing Practice - 5

## Model Answer - 5

Some people think students at schools and universities learn far more from lessons with teachers than from others sources (such as the internet, television).

Do you agree or disagree?

**In today's modern world there is no doubt that** we can now access seemingly limitless information from the Internet, television and the like. This has, therefore, questioned the relevance of teachers in schools and universities as a source of information for students. **Despite views to the contrary, I agree with the idea that** students still learn more effectively in a traditional learning environment with lessons provided by teachers rather than via media such as the Internet.

**The main reason why I agree is because** for many hundreds of years societies all over the world have been enriching the lives of people .by imparting their wisdom on them. While we do not all become pioneers like George Washington, Einstein and Gandhi we all have in common the fact that teachers helped pave the way for our future. While the implements of teaching and studying have changed over the years and led to such teaching tools as the active board and the Internet, none of them can replace the basic tool of teaching, the teacher.

**Another reason I agree is because** the teacher is able to focus on each student as an individual, monitoring progress and assessing areas of difficulty of each person in their class. This fine-tuning helps each student maximise the benefits they attain from each lesson. Without this, one student might find a class too easy and another too difficult. It is the teacher that creates the ability to judge what each student needs, an ability that the Internet does not have.

**In conclusion, I need to repeat my initial opinion that I am in agreement with the notion that** the Internet and other sources of information can not replace the traditional position filled by teachers as this tried and trusted method of teaching is both flexible and can change to the needs of the student and to the needs of society.

# Task 2 – Writing Practice - 6

## Model Answer - 6

Some people believe that museums and art galleries are not essential for a society and they should not be funded by the government. Others, however, believe that support from the government should be provided.

Discuss both these views and give your own opinion.

**While technology has certainly changed the way many people** seek entertainment the more traditional forms of visiting museums and art galleries still entice many people to visit. The dilemma arising from this, however, is whether or not such establishments should no longer be funded by the government. **In this essay I am going to examine this question from both points of view and then give my own opinion on the matter.**

**One obvious criticism of** funding museums and art galleries is that it takes money away from other needy aspects of society such as education and health. **It is difficult to justify** spending money on a painting that is worth millions of dollars when people are still leaving school unable to read properly and others suffer from illnesses that hospitals can not treat properly due to poor underfunded facilities.

**While these claims are valid** it is important to appreciate the importance of museums and similar institutions in providing not only secure premises to keep often priceless and unique artefacts from around the world but also generating money. A world famous museum or art gallery can attract millions of people both locally and internationally. This in turn helps to stimulate the local economy for small and large businesses providing jobs for many people.

**In conclusion, I believe both sides of the argument have their merits. On balance, however, I tend to believe that** the government should support museums and art galleries that need that extra help to survive. In time, these can develop into successful places that not only become a must visit institution for local residents but also those overseas who come to enjoy what they have to offer.

# Task 2 – Writing Practice - 7

## Model Answer - 7

Recycling is now an essential measure: it is time for everyone in society to become more responsible towards the environment.

To what extent do you agree or disagree with this statement?

Recycling **has become a part of everyday life for many people and has, therefore, encouraged many people to voice the opinion that** what happens to our planet should be the responsibility of everyone on it. **Despite views to the contrary, I totally agree with the idea that** everyone should be responsible for the earth that we live on and need to work actively and passionately to protect it.

**The main reason why I completely agree is because**, as members of an exclusive club of residents on this planet, we all use the resources available to us. We all need water for drinking, wood for building homes and furniture, the sun for warmth and energy and so on. However, if we assume that these resources are limitless we will one day wake up to realise we should have acted sooner but now it is too late. Luckily, we still have time and, step by step, we can all add to the protection of our planet.

**Another reason I completely agree is because**, through recycling, we can reduce the mountains of plastic, glass and aluminium that exist in many countries and feed these back into the many processes that use them. It is important to realise that the little done by each individual once multiplied by the millions of people doing the same thing can make a huge difference in resource usage.

**In conclusion, I need to repeat my initial opinion that I am in complete agreement with the notion that** we must all, in whatever way we can, help protect the environment. This could change from place to place depending on the situation and even the age of the person but a life time commitment to protecting where we live must be the focus of everyone.

# Task 2 – Writing Practice - 8

## Model Answer - 8

In many countries, more people than ever before drive private cars.

Do you think the advantages of this development outweigh the disadvantages?

**There is no doubt that in recent years** roads have become more and more congested because of a widespread increase in the number of private car owners. **While this has brought both positive and negative influences, I personally believe that the advantages outweigh the disadvantages and will present my reasons for this opinion in this essay.**

**The main advantage of** an increase in car ownership is that people become more independent of public transport and can control their schedules more easily. The weekly trip to the supermarket, for example, now becomes less of a chore as it can be done more comfortably, takes less time and requires little physical effort to carry the shopping bags. People can become more spontaneous as the decision to go somewhere no longer needs planning and so life can become more adventurous without the need to always worry about bus or train timetables and the weather.

**There are, however, undeniable disadvantages such as** rush hour which can become a frustrating time of day and has been seen to lead to a social phenomenon called road rage. While this is certainly an annoying situation it can often be avoided by adopting a more flexible working schedule allowing you to leave before or after the busy times. **Another possible problem is** the extra expense needed to maintain your car. This is something that can come at the most unexpected times and might place a strain on your finances.

**In conclusion, it seems clear that the advantages** of owning a car **outweigh any possible disadvantages because** the chance to become more independent and more spontaneous in your life is something that should be embraced rather than avoided. This is particularly true when you are young and have the energy and more disposable income to enjoy this freedom.

# Task 2 – Writing Practice - 9

## Model Answer – 9

The world is experiencing a dramatic increase in population. This is causing problems not only for poor, undeveloped countries, but also for industrialised and developing nations.

Describe some of the problems that overpopulation causes, and suggest at least one possible solution.

Overpopulation **has become a major issue in society in the 21st century** and is seen as negatively influencing not only poor countries but also developed countries. **The purpose of this essay is to look at some of the problems caused by overpopulation as well as offer a practical solution to this.**

**One undeniable problem caused by** an excessive population growth is a strain on available resources. Water is an obvious example as more is needed for not only human consumption but also the watering of crops, and industrial use. Demands for energy increase dramatically as well with more people using their own transport and factories manufacturing more goods for consumption. It is inevitable that more people leads to more demands and more waste and greater pollution in the world.

**One way to help address this issue would be for the government to impose** an upper limit to how many children a family can have. The one-child policy tried in China for years did work but also resulted in a wide disparity in males to females in many places. Tax incentives might also work with less tax being paid by parents with less children. This would be of benefit to any family finding it difficult to make ends meet as salaries rarely keep up with inflation.

**In conclusion**, it is clear that while not all countries are suffering from too many people, Japan is one example, all countries will nevertheless feel the effects of ever diminishing global resources if nothing is done. Government enforcement of a one-child policy can work but would almost certainly meet with public resistance in developed countries. However, tax incentives would find favour with many people and still offer them a choice of more children if they were willing to pay more.

# Task 2 – Writing Practice - 10

## Model Answer - 10

Some people feel that certain workers like nurses, doctors and teachers are undervalued and should be paid more, especially when other people like film actors and company bosses are paid huge sums of money that are out of proportion to the importance of the work that they do.

How far do you agree?
What criteria should be used to decide how much people are paid?

**It is common knowledge that** certain professions like film stars and corporate bosses earn far in excess of that earned by doctors, nurses and the like. **It is not unusual, therefore, to hear people argue that** certain professions should be paid less and others more to help reduce this huge difference in salary. **I am in total disagreement with this sentiment** and in this essay will explain why as well as discuss what criteria can help decide the salary of different professions.

**I completely disagree that** the salaries for certain professions are undervalued while others are paid excessively. **While there is no denying that** people like film stars and company bosses earn far more than most people can ever dream of, we also need to look at the 'hidden' benefits of their success. The revenue generated indirectly by a film star can come to billions of dollars and pays for the thousands of people employed in the making, distribution and promotion of the film. A nurse, on the other hand, as good as she or he is at helping patients, is more replaceable than a film star or business tycoon.

The criteria of how much money someone makes is not likely to change. For a star it is about how much money they can generate and so the sky really is the limit. For a nurse, however, a standard salary for a nurse with a predetermined level of experience and required qualification is not likely to change. High salary earners in the entertainment business often have agents who negotiate salaries for them but a nurses salary is often nonnegotiable. This is because people working alongside many people doing the same or similar job have to have uniformity. or chaos would ensue. Their way of negotiating is then often through a union rather than an agent.

**In conclusion, I completely disagree that** salaries need to be re-evaluated. While it might seem unfair that a business man can earn more in one year's bonus than most people earn in a life time the money they generate creates employment for many people. Equally, if a nurse was paid far more than she gets now the health service in most countries would collapse as most people would not be able to afford their services.

## Writing Test Score Sheet

Task 2 score →

| Task 1 score ↓ | 0 | 0.5 | 1.0 | 1.5 | 2.0 | 2.5 | 3.0 | 3.5 | 4.0 | 4.5 | 5.0 | 5.5 | 6.0 | 6.5 | 7.0 | 7.5 | 8.0 | 8.5 | 9.0 |
|---|---|---|---|---|---|---|---|---|---|---|---|---|---|---|---|---|---|---|---|
| 0   | 0   | 0.5 | 1   | 1   | 1   | 1.5 | 2   | 2.5 | 3   | 3   | 3   | 3.5 | 4   | 4.5 | 5   | 5   | 5   | 5.5 | 6 |
| 0.5 | 0   | 0.5 | 1   | 1.5 | 1.5 | 1.5 | 2   | 2.5 | 3   | 3   | 3.5 | 3.5 | 4   | 4.5 | 5   | 5.5 | 5.5 | 5.5 | 6 |
| 1.0 | 0   | 0.5 | 1   | 1.5 | 2   | 2   | 2   | 2.5 | 3   | 3.5 | 4   | 4   | 4   | 4.5 | 5   | 5.5 | 6   | 6   | 6 |
| 1.5 | 0.5 | 0.5 | 1   | 1.5 | 2   | 2.5 | 2.5 | 2.5 | 3   | 3.5 | 4   | 4.5 | 4.5 | 4.5 | 5   | 5.5 | 6   | 6.5 | 6.5 |
| 2.0 | 1   | 1   | 1   | 1.5 | 2   | 2.5 | 3   | 3   | 3   | 3.5 | 4   | 4.5 | 5   | 5   | 5   | 5.5 | 6   | 6.5 | 7 |
| 2.5 | 1   | 1.5 | 1.5 | 1.5 | 2   | 2.5 | 3   | 3.5 | 3.5 | 3.5 | 4   | 4.5 | 5   | 5.5 | 5.5 | 5.5 | 6   | 6.5 | 7 |
| 3.0 | 1   | 1.5 | 2   | 2   | 2   | 2.5 | 3   | 3.5 | 4   | 4   | 4   | 4.5 | 5   | 5.5 | 6   | 6   | 6   | 6.5 | 7 |
| 3.5 | 1   | 1.5 | 2   | 2.5 | 2.5 | 2.5 | 3   | 3.5 | 4   | 4.5 | 4.5 | 4.5 | 5   | 5.5 | 6   | 6.5 | 6.5 | 6.5 | 7 |
| 4.0 | 1   | 1.5 | 2   | 2.5 | 3   | 3   | 3   | 3.5 | 4   | 4.5 | 5   | 5   | 5   | 5.5 | 6   | 6.5 | 7   | 7   | 7 |
| 4.5 | 1.5 | 1.5 | 2   | 2.5 | 3   | 3.5 | 3.5 | 3.5 | 4   | 4.5 | 5   | 5.5 | 5.5 | 5.5 | 6   | 6.5 | 7   | 7.5 | 7.5 |
| 5.0 | 2   | 2   | 2   | 2.5 | 3   | 3.5 | 4   | 4   | 4   | 4.5 | 5   | 5.5 | 6   | 6   | 6   | 6.5 | 7   | 7.5 | 8 |
| 5.5 | 2   | 2   | 2.5 | 2.5 | 3   | 3.5 | 4   | 4.5 | 4.5 | 4.5 | 5   | 5.5 | 6   | 6.5 | 6.5 | 6.5 | 7   | 7.5 | 8 |
| 6.0 | 2   | 2.5 | 2.5 | 3   | 3   | 3.5 | 4   | 4.5 | 5   | 5   | 5   | 5.5 | 6   | 6.5 | 7   | 7   | 7   | 7.5 | 8 |
| 6.5 | 2   | 2.5 | 3   | 3   | 3.5 | 3.5 | 4   | 4.5 | 5   | 5.5 | 5.5 | 5.5 | 6   | 6.5 | 7   | 7.5 | 7.5 | 7.5 | 8 |
| 7.0 | 2   | 2.5 | 3   | 3.5 | 3.5 | 4   | 4   | 4.5 | 5   | 5.5 | 6   | 6   | 6   | 6.5 | 7   | 7.5 | 8   | 8   | 8 |
| 7.5 | 2.5 | 2.5 | 3   | 3.5 | 4   | 4   | 4.5 | 4.5 | 5   | 5.5 | 6   | 6.5 | 6.5 | 6.5 | 7   | 7.5 | 8   | 8.5 | 8.5 |
| 8.0 | 3   | 3   | 3   | 3.5 | 4   | 4.5 | 5   | 5   | 5   | 5.5 | 6   | 6.5 | 7   | 7   | 7   | 7.5 | 8   | 8.5 | 9 |
| 8.5 | 3   | 3   | 3.5 | 3.5 | 4   | 4.5 | 5   | 5.5 | 5.5 | 5.5 | 6   | 6.5 | 7   | 7.5 | 7.5 | 7.5 | 8   | 8.5 | 9 |
| 9.0 | 3   | 3.5 | 4   | 4   | 4   | 4.5 | 5   | 5.5 | 6   | 6   | 6   | 6.5 | 7   | 7.5 | 8   | 8   | 8   | 8.5 | 9 |

If you scored grade 6.0 for Task 2 and grade 5.5 for Task 1, the overall grade is 6.0

However, if you scored grade 5.5 for Task 2 and grade 6.0 for Task 1, the overall grade is 5.5

This is known as a weighted average with Task 2 being given more influence over your final grade.

# ANSWERS

# ANSWERS

Page 8

| Opinion led |
|---|
| 5 |
| 6 |
| 9 |
| 10 |
|  |

| Argument led |
|---|
| 3 |
| 4 |
| 1 - is possible |
|  |
|  |

| Two questions |
|---|
| 1 |
| 2 |
| 7 |
| 8 |
|  |

1. Advantages / Disadvantages
2. Cause / Solution
3. Discuss both points of view and give your own opinion
4. Discuss the advantages and disadvantages and give your own opinion
5. Do the advantages outweigh the disadvantages?
6. Do you agree or disagree?
7. Opinion / Solution
8. Problem / Solution
9. To what extent do you agree or disagree?
10. What is your opinion?


Page 44
Introduction

**Answer**

**Many scholars are now convinced that** future wars will be triggered by a lack of land, food and water rather than for political reasons. One of the main causes of this is likely to be the global population explosion. It is, **therefore**, essential that ways to help control this are put into action before it is too late. **This essay first looks at possible problems of this phenomenon and then offers** several suggestions to help make inroads into this problem.

# Essay Analysis - Pages 53 - 57

**NOTE:** The underlined words show the grammar errors and the bold words show the vocabulary errors.

The social media has been paying particular attention in recent years to a disturbing **phenomena** of a negative attitude in many students graduating **form** university. The purpose of this essay is to looking at some of the causes of negativity in school graduates.

It is difficult to **refuse** the fact that social media in all its guises has contribute to students feeling rather **pesimistic** about their future. When students are constantly bombarded with information about natural resources running out, environmental pollution, war in different countries around the world and high unemployment, it is, perhaps, understandable if after hearing all of these negatives that students pick up on this and also feel negative about life.

We can start to alter this issue by students exposing to more optimistic view of the university. This can be done by instilling into each student the belief that they are in charge of their destiny regardless of what is **happens** in the world. This can also be achieved by focusing on role models who have made a success of their lives despite coming from humble beginnings and having seemingly impossible **hurdle** to cross before they could have success.

In summary, with access to more media than in any previous generation students are constantly surrounded by positive views of the world and by reflection their future. To balance this schools need to present what appears to be taboo to presenters of daily news and that is good news. Having guest lecturers at the school, showing motivational movies and using inspirational books as reading projects will help students see that life is a mix of good and bad and will help ensure they remain motivated after graduating.

www.ingramcontent.com/pod-product-compliance
Lightning Source LLC
Chambersburg PA
CBHW080523110426
42742CB00017B/3219